Intelligence
Linda Wasmer Andrews

Franklin Watts
A Division of Scholastic Inc.
New York • Toronto • London • Auckland • Sydney
Mexico City • New Delhi • Hong Kong
Danbury, Connecticut

Dedication
For David Lee, who was smart enough to pick me.

Cover Illustration by Peter Cho
Cover and Interior Design by Kathleen Santini
Illustrations by Pat Rasch

Library of Congress Cataloging-in-Publication Data

Andrews, Linda Wasmer.
  Intelligence / Linda Wasmer Andrews.
      p. cm.—(Life balance)
Summary: Examines various theories and types of intelligence, including a look at historical studies and people who have made significant contributions to the field.
Includes bibliographical references and index.
  ISBN 0-531-12220-4 (lib. bdg.)   0-531-16608-2 (pbk.)
  1. Intellect—Juvenile literature. [1. Intellect.] I. Title. II. Series.
  BF431.A576 2003
  153.9—dc21
                                    2003000023

Copyright © 2003 by Scholastic Inc.
All rights reserved. Published simultaneously in Canada.
Printed in the United States of America.
1 2 3 4 5 6 7 8 9 10 R 12 11 10 09 08 07 06 05 04 03

Table of Contents

Chapter One	Intelligence: Fact and Fiction	5
Chapter Two	Single-Minded: The *g* Factor	17
Chapter Three	New Ideas: Other Intelligences	31
Chapter Four	Smart Question: Nature or Nurture?	43
Chapter Five	Testing, Testing: The IQ Debate	57
	Glossary	69
	Further Resources	72
	Index	76
	About the Author	80

One
Intelligence: Fact and Fiction

Student X always knows the answer when the teacher calls on her in class. She gets straight A's on her report card and rarely misses a question on tests. She has won prizes in the school spelling bee and the city science fair. Recently, she was chosen for a gifted program that lets her take high-school classes while still in middle school.

Student Y has a lot of trouble paying attention in class. He always seems to be daydreaming when he should be listening, or doodling in his notebook when he should be doing schoolwork. The other students often make fun of him. Once, he overheard the teacher saying that it wasn't worthwhile for him to even be in school.

Which student is intelligent? If you said Student X, you're correct. Every school has bright, hard-working star students. No one doubts that they're smart. However, if you said Student Y, you may also be correct. In fact, this is a description of young Thomas Edison. His teacher called him "addled," or confused, because he tended to daydream during class and doodle in his notebook. Edison lasted only about three months in school. Yet he went on to become one of the most successful inventors in history. Among other things, he developed practical electric lighting and invented the phonograph.

Artificial Intelligence: Science or Science Fiction?

Today, there are computer programs and robots that can use information to make choices. The more information they receive, the better decisions they make. Does this mean the machines are intelligent? Some people think so. In fact, this is what the field of artificial intelligence is all about. Scientists try to develop machines that can "learn" new information, then use it for some purpose. There are already computer programs that can play chess or make decisions about which people are most likely to repay their bank loans. Still, no current machine comes close to being able to think like a human. Many tasks that are easy for humans to perform have proved to be huge hurdles for machines. Examples include recognizing a face or feeling an emotion.

Different people use the word *intelligence* to mean different things. One common definition is the ability to learn and then put that learning to good use. By this definition, a straight-A student who learns in the classroom and then uses that knowledge to get good grades would fit the bill. Yet, so would a C student who learns by tinkering at home and then uses that knowledge to build a better skateboard. It's a myth that honor roll students are the only intelligent ones in school.

More Myths and Truths

There are many other false ideas about intelligence. Some myths have been repeated so often that people start to believe they are true. Here are some of the most common ones.

Myth: Doctors and scientists are smart. Models and athletes aren't. And almost everybody else falls somewhere in between.

Truth: It's true that a certain amount of brainpower is needed to become a brain surgeon or a rocket scientist. Yet there are highly intelligent people in every walk of life. Just look at the membership of Mensa, an international club for people who get high scores on standard tests of intelligence. Mensa members include professors and prizewinners. However, they also include truck drivers, firefighters,

> **Who Am I?**
>
> *Question:* I have an IQ of 154, which rates me as highly gifted. I started college when I was just fifteen. Who am I?
>
> A. Bill Gates, computer whiz
> B. Sharon Stone, movie star
> C. Sandra Day O'Connor, Supreme Court justice
> D. Kobe Bryant, basketball star
>
> *Answer:* The joke is on people who tell blond jokes. The answer is B—beautiful, blond actress Sharon Stone. You can't judge intelligence by the color of a person's hair, eyes, or skin.

police officers, artists, musicians, and farmers. Two well-known current members are Ellen Morphonios, a former model who is now a judge, and Bobby Czyz, a former boxing champion who is now a sports announcer.

Myth: Intelligence and IQ are the same thing.

Truth: IQ—short for intelligence quotient—refers to the score received on a standard test of intelligence. But it's quite possible to have a high IQ, yet not put that mental ability to good use by studying or working hard. It's also possible to be intelligent, yet not get a high IQ score. For example, if you're feeling sick on the test day, you may have trouble concentrating on the questions. You might end up with a score that is far below what you would have gotten on another day. Or, if the test is written in English, but you grew up speaking another language, once again your score might not reveal your true intelligence. Another problem that might arise is if the particular test you're taking doesn't happen to measure the kinds of things you do best.

Myth: Bigger is better when it comes to brains.

Truth: The brain is the control center for intelligence. As a general rule, people with large brains tend to score a little higher than average on IQ tests. However, there are many exceptions to this, so the person with the biggest brain isn't always the smartest. Think of a school bus compared to a sports car. The bus may be bigger, but the car is faster and more streamlined. It's the same with brains. It's not so much a matter of how big they are but how well they run. Scientists have found that the brains of "brainy" people tend to send messages from one nerve cell to another more quickly than usual. They also tend to use less energy while solving problems.

A PET scan—short for positron-emission tomography—is an image that shows the brain in action. It is one tool scientists use for understanding how the brain works. Scientists have long known that people use different parts of their brains for different activities, which is another reason total brain size isn't as important as you might think. Using PET scans, scientists can see which parts of the brain "light up" during certain tasks.

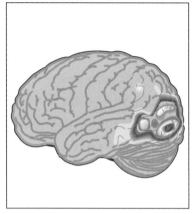
1. Seeing words

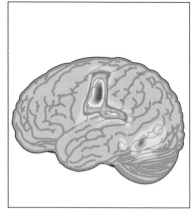
2. Speaking words

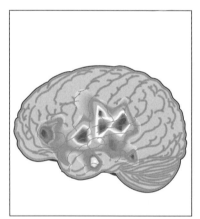
3. Hearing words

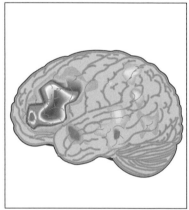
4. Thinking about words

The images above show parts of the brain that are active when people use words in various ways.

Myth: The mental abilities you need for reading, writing, and arithmetic are the only ones that count.

Truth: People who are good at using words and numbers tend to do well in school. However, there are many other skills that play a role in success. One popular theory is called multiple intelligences. It expands the idea of intelligence to include not just language abilities and number skills but also other kinds of "intelligences." Based on this theory, a musician might rely heavily on musical intelligence—the ability to recognize and create musical pitches, tones, and rhythms. A dancer might depend more on bodily-kinesthetic intelligence—the ability to use the mind to coordinate the body's movements. And a counselor might need a lot of interpersonal intelligence—the ability to understand the feelings and goals of other people. Another theory stresses the importance of practical intelligence. This is similar to common sense or "street smarts."

Myth: A person's skill at doing a particular mental task stays the same, no matter what the situation.

Truth: Just because you have trouble performing a task on a test doesn't mean you won't be able to do it in everyday life. For example, one study looked at poor Brazilian children. These children, who had little schooling, spent their days selling fruit on street corners or in open markets. They were able to solve tough math problems dealing with the price of fruit—for instance, if one melon costs 35 cruzeiros (the basic unit of money in Brazil), how much do six melons cost? But when they were asked to solve the same problems in formal arithmetic, for instance—what is 35 x 6?—most were unable to solve the problems correctly. Clearly, the children were capable of understanding numbers. However, for many, this ability was limited to a specific situation and didn't carry over to a school-like test.

Of Dummies and Nerds

Think about people you know who gain recognition for their achievements. Some are likely to be at the top of their class. Others are probably so-so students who were elected captain of their sports team, won a starring role in the school play, or started a fund-raising drive to raise money for charity. Obviously, these are no dummies. Instead, they're people who have learned a valuable skill and then used it well.

That's not to say that mental abilities aren't important. In fact, everyone can gain from learning to think more clearly and make better decisions. Yet intelligence often is misunderstood. Some students place too much stress on the kinds of mental abilities needed for school, acting as if getting straight A's is all that matters in life. Others place too little emphasis, talking about intelligence as if it were a disease. Many bright kids even try to play dumb. In many cases, it's because they're afraid of being called a nerd. One of the biggest myths about intelligence is that smart people are misfits who wear funny-looking clothes and trip over their own feet.

> ### It's SuperKid!
> *Melissa is a typical fifteen-year-old girl, except that she is already going to college—three years earlier than most teenagers. She is taking five college courses: physics, trigonometry, Spanish, history, and English. Even in college, Melissa stands out as a bright student. So what's her pet peeve? "People think everything comes easily for you if you're gifted," she says. "But even if you're smart, you still have to study."*
>
> *Now that she's in college, Melissa is hard to miss because she looks younger than everyone else. The attention can be embarrassing at times. "I'm a really shy person," she says. "And I have trouble making friends here." As you get to know Melissa, it becomes clear that she's really no superkid—just a kid with some super abilities mixed in with ordinary abilities and problems.*

Back in 1922, psychologist Lewis Terman decided to find out the truth. He began studying a group of more than 1,500 highly gifted children, nicknamed the Termites. It turned out to be the longest-running survey ever done. In fact, although Terman himself died in 1956, other researchers are still keeping tabs on the remaining Termites.

This study showed that most bright children are happy and well rounded. As the Termites grew up, they continued to thrive as a group. Most of them were relatively healthy, successful, and content with their lives.

By modern standards, Terman's study had flaws. For example, Terman haphazardly picked the children he studied. As a result, his group included more boys than girls and only two African Americans. Terman also meddled in the lives of

Termite Facts to Chew On

The people who took part in Lewis Terman's study have been researched more than almost any other group. Here are some fun facts about the Termites:

- *Two Termites made names for themselves in Hollywood as adults. Jess Oppenheimer was the creator of* I Love Lucy, *one of the best-loved television shows of all time. Edward Dmytryk directed twenty-three films, including* The Caine Mutiny, *a classic 1954 movie starring Humphrey Bogart.*
- *Another Termite who became famous was Ancel Keys. He was the scientist who discovered the link between cholesterol and heart disease.*
- *None of the Termites ever won a Nobel Prize, an important award for those who contribute greatly to culture or science. However, two bright children who were tested for the study but failed to make the cut did go on to win the Nobel Prize in physics: William Shockley in 1956 and Luis Alvarez in 1968.*

the children as they grew up. While he may have helped some to succeed, he also may have changed the outcome of his research. Still, the study went a long way toward dispelling the false belief that smart people are all "geeks."

Finally, it's also a myth that everyone agrees on the nature of intelligence. In truth, there are still many unanswered questions. For example, is intelligence one thing or many? Is it something you're born with or something you develop? Are IQ tests really a good way of measuring intelligence? These are some of the things you'll read about in the rest of this book.

Two
Single-Minded: The g Factor

Some people's brains just seem to work better and faster than others. We call these people intelligent, smart, bright, quick-witted, clever, or sharp—but what do we really mean? Is intelligence a single, wide-ranging ability that makes it easier to learn and do lots of things? Or is what we call intelligence really many separate abilities? This question has kept scientists busy for the last century.

In 1904, a British psychologist named Charles Spearman published a famous research paper in which he looked at children's scores in various school subjects. He found that children who got high scores in one subject tended to do well in other subjects, too. Likewise, children who did poorly tended to do so across the board. Spearman believed this was due to a general factor in human intelligence, which he called *g*.

> ### Plato Waxes Poetic on g
> Long before Spearman named g, people noticed that some folks just seemed sharper than others. An ancient Greek philosopher named Plato described intelligence as being like a block of wax; some people have a big block, others a small one. The blocks may also differ in hardness. If the wax is too hard, it may be difficult to press anything into it, and he or she may have difficulty learning. On the other hand, if the wax is too soft, it may not hold an impression. This person may have trouble with memory.

To understand this idea, it helps to imagine *g* as a large umbrella, symbolizing a single, broad mental capability. A number of narrower abilities can stand underneath this umbrella. For example, it might cover vocabulary, logic skills, problem-solving abilities, and so on.

Since Spearman's day, the notion of *g* has gained wide acceptance. Ninety years after his paper was published, more than fifty scientists banded together to sign a public statement on the matter. They noted that general intelligence is more than just one narrow skill. Instead, they agreed that it is a broader and deeper capability for "'catching on,' 'making sense' of things, and 'figuring out' what to do." Today, most scientists agree that *g* exists. However, some think it's the one true form of intelligence, while others think it's only one of many forms.

A Mental Pecking Order

Once you know about *g,* the next question is: Which specific abilities does it cover? In order to answer this question, scientists first made their best guesses about the kinds of mental abilities that might be involved. Then they developed tests for these abilities and used the tests in hundreds of studies. The goal was to see which abilities tended to be related to one another. For example, if people who scored high on one test also tended to score high on two other tests, it might be that all three abilities were related to each other. In other words, all three might be parts of *g.*

But there was a problem: Various researchers chose to use different types of tests. Also, the people tested were from a variety of ages and backgrounds. In addition, the researchers used different methods to analyze their findings and reach their conclusions. All of these approaches made it hard to compare the results from one study with another. It was like comparing apples with oranges.

Test Your Intelligence

Items such as the ones below are used to test for specific abilities that are thought to be parts of *g*. These are similar to the tasks you might be asked to do on some common tests of mental ability.

1. Tell how a starling and a lark are alike.

2. Name the capital of Mexico.

3. Underline the word that doesn't belong:
    puppy   kitten   horse   chick   calf

4. Find the missing detail in this picture:

5. Pick the shape that comes next.

Choose one:

6. Write the numbers that come next:
    1, 5, 3, 7, 5, 9, ___, ___

7. Solve this word problem:
    Jane is taller than Susan but shorter than Mark. Susan is taller than Bill. Who is shortest?

Answers: (1) they're both birds; (2) Mexico City; (3) horse; (4) the pedals are missing; (5) C; (6) 7, 11; (7) Bill

A real intelligence test would include more items assessing a wider range of knowledge and skills. The above test is meant just for fun, so your score doesn't actually tell you how smart you are. These examples also give you a chance to practice the kinds of tasks that you might need to do on an actual test someday. Being familiar with the tasks may make it easier to do your best when it counts.

Yet despite this tangle of facts, some common threads have been found. First, people who do well on one test of mental ability also tend to do well on others. This observation can be explained by *g*, the broad mental capability that makes some people better than others at mental tasks in general.

Second, certain kinds of mental abilities are more closely linked than other kinds. For example, people who get high scores on a test that involves repeating a string of numbers are likely to also do well on any other mental test. However, they are *especially* likely to score well on a test that involves solving math problems in their head. Similarly, people who ace a vocabulary test are especially likely to also do well on a test of knowledge about people, places, and events. In other words, mental abilities tend to cluster into groups based on related skills, such as being good with numbers or words.

In 1993, an American psychologist named John Carroll published a massive book called *Human Cognitive Abilities.* In his book, Carroll reviewed more than four hundred studies that had been done by scores of different scientists over the years. All of the studies involved some kind of mental test. As a result of his review, Carroll proposed a three-level model of intelligence. The top level is *g*. The second level consists of eight groups of mental abilities:

- the ability to understand and use new information

- a person's fund of general knowledge

- the ability to learn and remember information

- the ability to deal with information that is seen

- the ability to deal with information that is heard

- the ability to call up information from memory

- the ability to perform mental tasks quickly

- the ability to react to information quickly

The third level consists of the specific abilities within each group (see the chart on pages 24-25).

Carroll's model is important because it sums up nearly a century's worth of research on *g*. The idea that there is such a thing as general intelligence has been influential. It led to the development of modern intelligence tests. It caused some people to be labeled smart and others not. And it continues to have an impact on the way that most people think about intelligence today.

Three Levels of Intelligence

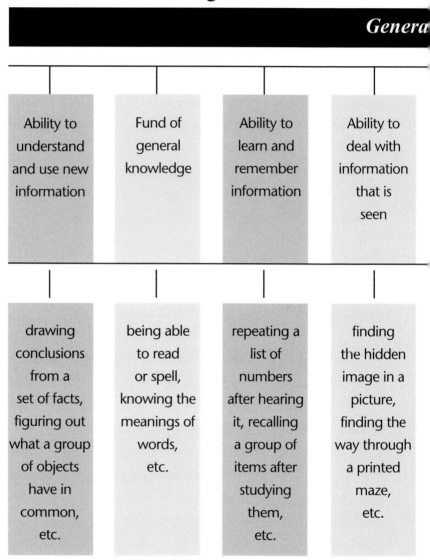

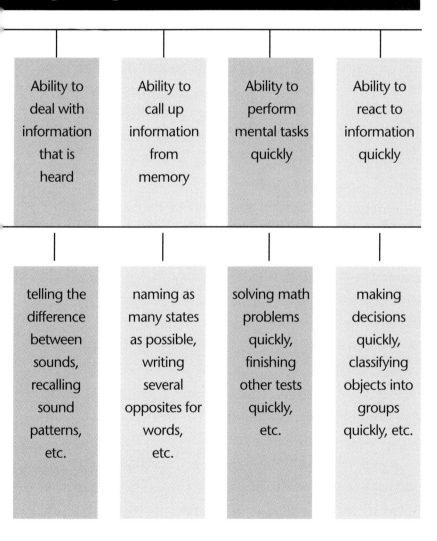

To *g* or Not to *g*

Not everyone buys this view of intelligence, however. For one thing, the theory is only as good as the tests it is based on. The tests used to assess *g* look at specific mental abilities. Yet these are only parts of what makes up intelligence, not the whole thing. In addition, some tests consist of rather odd tasks, such as repeating a list of numbers forward and backward. Such tasks are chosen because they are quick to do and easy to score. However, they are only indirectly related to real-world tasks, such as writing an essay or designing a machine.

A second problem is that the tests only look at those parts of intelligence that our society values. For example, two of Carroll's categories have to do with speed, a quality that is highly valued in American life. Ours is a culture in which people always seem to be racing from one activity to the next, and even young children frequently are urged to "hurry up." In many cultures, though, the stress is on thinking deeply rather than quickly. Work that is done too rapidly may even be suspected of being careless and sloppy. A test that takes off points for answering slowly may work against people who have been raised to take their time.

A third problem is that people who learn test-taking tricks often can boost their scores a bit. To some degree, then, the tests may be measuring not how smart people are, but just how good they are at taking tests. These problems don't necessarily mean that *g* doesn't exist. They might mean that scientists haven't yet found a perfect way of measuring it.

> ### The Ultimate g
> Say the word "genius," and people often think of Albert Einstein, the wild-haired German scientist. His ideas changed the way modern scientists think about space and time. When Einstein died in 1955, his brain was removed and preserved. In 1999, Canadian researchers published new findings about it. Einstein's brain was about average in size. However, the part that controls math and the ability to create mental images was 15 percent wider than average. This area of his brain also may have had an unusually large number of connections among cells. That could help explain Einstein's fabled ability to use his imagination to solve math problems. For example, he came up with his famous theory of relativity after imagining what it would be like to ride through space on a beam of light.

Despite their flaws, tests of mental ability have proved useful. They have helped scientists establish some handy rules of thumb for human intelligence. Remember, though, that any person may be the exception to the rule. For example, people who do well on Test A may also tend to do well on Test B. When it comes to you in particular, however, there are no guarantees. Maybe you're better at solving problems with numbers rather than words. Or maybe you skipped breakfast on the day of the second test. There are all kinds of reasons why anybody might wind up getting different scores on two different mental tests.

Finally, there are lots of valuable abilities that most tests don't even try to measure. These include artistic talent and common sense. As a result, such abilities have been omitted from most theories of intelligence. Recently, though, some scientists have started to pay more attention to these abilities. Their ideas are discussed in the next chapter.

Your Own Definition

What do *you* think intelligence is? Try this experiment: List the three abilities that come to your mind first when you hear the word "intelligence." Ask several classmates to do the same. Then compare lists. Chances are, there will be a number of differences, even though you are all the same age, live in the same place, go to the same school, and probably have many experiences in common.

Now imagine comparing lists with someone who lives halfway around the world and who has had a very different life from your own. It's likely that the differences would be even greater. The fact is, people's ideas about which abilities make up intelligence are greatly affected by the beliefs of their culture.

For example, in our society, we tend to think of a smart person as someone who spends a lot of time studying and who enjoys learning. In traditional Chinese culture, however, the stress is on knowing yourself as well as learning about the world. Even today, researchers have found that Chinese people, unlike Americans, often list self-knowledge as one key aspect of intelligence.

Studies from Africa offer yet another window on the subject. In Zimbabwe, the word for intelligence *(ngware)* actually means to be wise and careful, particularly in relationships with other people. In Zambia, too, being intelligent means having social skills, such as being dutiful and cooperative.

It's worth noting these different ideas about what intelligence means. The concept of *g* has a long history in our culture, and it has been well researched in scientific studies. Still, no one theory holds all the answers. In truth, there are many definitions of intelligence, and each one has something to teach us.

Three
New Ideas: Other Intelligences

As a teenager, Chris set his sights on being an actor. His big break came at age twenty-one, when he won a role in a television movie. Although the part was small, his talent was noticed. A couple of years later, he was chosen to star in a television series. The show ran from 1989 to 1993, and during this time, it received rave reviews from the critics. Today, Chris still acts occasionally. He also tours the country, singing and dancing with a band.

That would be impressive success for anyone. What makes it even more remarkable is that Chris Burke has Down syndrome. This is a genetic disorder that can cause a number of physical signs, including upward-slanting eyes and a flat-looking face. It also sometimes causes poor muscle tone or problems with the heart, stomach, or eyes. In addition, most people with the condition have some degree of mental retardation. This means that their intelligence, as measured by an IQ test, is well below average. It also means that they have trouble functioning in everyday life and keeping up with other people their age.

Obviously, IQ alone doesn't tell the whole story about Chris. He has other things going for him—such as talent and a winning personality—that IQ tests don't measure. These other abilities are valuable skills that are controlled by the mind. Does that mean they are forms of intelligence? Some scientists think so. They argue that there are clusters of important mental abilities that are completely separate from g.

Other scientists agree that these are useful abilities. However, they prefer to label these skills as special talents rather than types of intelligence. One concern is that there aren't good tests for measuring many of these abilities. As a result, it's hard to study them scientifically the way word and number skills have been studied. Whatever term you use, though, these skills are clearly important. For many people, they may be the secrets to success in life.

> ### *Passing the Test of Life*
> *These movers and shakers struggled with school and tests but got an A+ in life:*
> - *Winston Churchill, British prime minister and winner of the Nobel Prize for literature—was last in his class at school.*
> - *Robert Jarvik, American doctor who invented the first permanent artificial heart—was rejected by fifteen medical schools.*
> - *John F. Kennedy, American president—received reports of "poor achievement" in school and had trouble with spelling.*
> - *Isaac Newton, English scientist who invented calculus and discovered the secrets of gravity, light, and color—was a poor student.*
> - *George Washington, American president—had dyslexia, a learning disorder that affects a person's ability to read, write, and spell.*

Multiple Intelligences

In 1983, Howard Gardner, a professor of education at Harvard University, published a book called *Frames of Mind*. In the book, he described his theory of multiple intelligences. This theory has since become popular with teachers because it doesn't just focus on one or two ways of learning. Instead, it embraces a wide range of learning styles. Gardner thinks there are several different "intelligences" that are separate but equal in the mind. Let's say a class is studying plants. Some students might learn best by reading a book about plants, others by raising a garden. Either way of learning is equally valid, according to this view. So far, Gardner has named eight types of intelligence:

- *Linguistic intelligence* is the ability to use words well. You might call this "word smart." Lawyers, public speakers, reporters, and writers use this skill.

- *Logical-mathematical intelligence* is the ability to think logically and use numbers well. You might call this "number smart." Bookkeepers, computer programmers, mathematicians, and scientists use this skill.

- *Spatial intelligence* is the ability to create mental images in order to solve problems. You might call this "picture smart." Architects, artists, engineers, and navigators use this skill.

- *Musical intelligence* is the ability to recognize and create musical pitches, tones, and rhythms. You might call this "music smart." Composers, dancers, musicians, and singers use this skill.

- *Bodily-kinesthetic intelligence* is the ability to use the mind to coordinate the body's movements. You might call this "body smart." Athletes, dancers, mechanics, and surgeons use this skill.

- *Naturalist intelligence* is the ability to recognize different plants and animals. You might call this "nature smart." Farmers, fishermen, forest rangers, and natural scientists use this skill.

- *Interpersonal intelligence* is the ability to understand the feelings and goals of other people. You might call this "people smart." Actors, counselors, managers, and teachers use this skill.

- *Intrapersonal intelligence* is the ability to understand your own feelings and goals. You might call this "self smart." Everyone uses this skill.

Gardner believes that everybody who isn't disabled has all of these intelligences to some degree. However, people vary widely in their strengths and weaknesses. For example, one person might be strong in musical ability but weak in people skills. Another person might be just the opposite.

> ### What's Your EQ?
> *Emotional intelligence—sometimes called EQ, for emotional quotient—is another hot new idea. Think of it as a mixture of being "self smart" and "people smart." It involves knowing and handling your own feelings and goals. It also involves dealing with other people and understanding their feelings. The popularity of this idea is based on a fact of life: As adults, some very brainy people never take off in their careers. On the other hand, some less brainy people do quite well. What makes the difference? In many cases, it may be emotional skills. Such skills help people stay motivated at work, make calm business decisions, and get along well with coworkers and customers.*

Linguistic intelligence and logical-mathematical intelligence are the same types of abilities that IQ tests measure. They are also the skills that schools stress the most. However, the other intelligences that Gardner describes go far beyond book smarts. Everyone knows kids who have problems with reading, writing, and arithmetic, yet who shine in art or music class or on a sports team. Gardner's theory provides a framework for understanding and building on these other skills. His theory still needs more testing in scientific studies. Still, it holds a lot of appeal because it offers a way of thinking about a wide range of abilities.

At some schools, these ideas are already changing the way teachers teach. The goal is to help students use all their abilities to the fullest. Let's say you're studying about oceans. You might be asked to write a report about sea life, using your word skills. Or you might be asked to figure out how long it would take a ship to cross the ocean, using your number skills. These are pretty typical lessons. However, you also might draw a picture of fish, using your picture skills. You might tap glasses containing different amounts of water, using your music skills. You might move like a dolphin, using your body skills. You might identify seashells, using your nature skills. You might design a ship with a group of students, using your people skills. And you might pick your favorite sea creature and tell why you like it, using your self skills.

Practical Intelligence

The theory of multiple intelligences covers a lot of ground. Something is still missing, though. What about abilities such as common sense and "street smarts"? That's where practical intelligence comes in. The man behind this idea is Robert Sternberg, a psychologist at Yale University. For him, practical intelligence is the ability to understand and solve real-life problems. He says it's one of three keys to success in life. The others are creativity and the kind of intelligence measured on IQ tests.

Gifts That Keep Giving

Giftedness and intelligence may go hand in hand, but they aren't exactly the same thing. Intelligence is a term used to describe people of all ages in all kinds of situations. Giftedness, on the other hand, is a term that is often used for students who have the capability to excel in school. The exact nature of giftedness, like the nature of intelligence itself, is still being debated. However, giftedness is usually thought to include several abilities that are similar to Gardner's intelligences.

Each state makes its own rules about which students can take part in gifted classes. In most cases, the states are guided by a definition set by the United States government. It says giftedness is the capability for high performance in one or more key areas. Gifted students also need special school programs to make the most of their abilities. These are some areas in which students may be gifted:

- general intelligence—Getting high scores on intelligence tests. This often involves being smart about words and numbers.

- academics—Doing well in school subjects. This often involves being smart about words and numbers as well.

- leadership—Being a leader within a group. This often involves being smart about yourself and other people.

- arts—Being talented in art, dance, music, or drama. This often involves being smart about pictures, music, or the way you use your body.

- creativity—Coming up with creative ideas. This involves using your talent in another area in clever new ways.

Sternberg points out that no one is good at everything. What sets apart successful people, he says, is that they know their strong and weak points. They then build on their strengths. They also learn how to fix or make up for their weaknesses. You can do this, too. Let's say you know you're good at working with your hands, and you enjoy tinkering with gadgets more than reading or doing math. When you get to high school, you might sign up for auto shop. However, to work on cars, you'll have to read repair manuals and know which size tools to use, so you'll need to sharpen your reading and math skills as well. The goal is to make the most of all your abilities.

Here are some more tips adapted from Sternberg's book *Successful Intelligence:*

- Want to do your best. It doesn't matter how much brains and talent you have if you don't care enough to use them.
- Don't act on impulse. Sometimes you have to think fast. More often, though, it pays to think through a problem or decision.
- Don't give up too soon. When you're trying something new, you'll never get anywhere if you quit at the first sign of difficulty.
- Turn thoughts into action. It's not enough simply to have good ideas. You also need to act on them to achieve anything.

- Be willing to risk failure. Everyone fails now and then. Just learn from your mistakes, and don't keep repeating them.
- Don't take on too much or too little. Aim for a balance between spreading yourself too thin and doing less than you could.
- Don't put things off. If you wait until the last minute to do something, you probably won't do your best. Plan your time wisely.

By trying these tips, you might even discover abilities you didn't know you had. Sternberg himself is a great example of this. He says that, as a young child, he was considered a "dum-dum." His IQ test scores were low and so were his grades. It wasn't until he reached fourth grade that he had a teacher who helped him believe in himself. Soon, he was an A student. Today, this former dum-dum teaches at one of the top universities in the country. He is also the author of more than forty books and a leading expert on intelligence.

The moral: IQ may be important, but it certainly isn't everything. Each person has a unique mix of skills and talents. Some are measured by standard intelligence tests and some aren't. But no one's potential can be summed up by a single test score.

Four
Smart Question: Nature or Nurture?

Wolfgang Amadeus Mozart, the eighteenth-century Austrian composer, was one of the greatest musical geniuses of all time. By any measure, he was a bright child. He liked numbers, and he picked up languages easily. However, his mental abilities were most obvious when it came to music. He began to play piano at age three. By age five, he was writing his own pieces. When he was six, he played for the Austrian empress at her court. By his teens, Mozart was composing great music that showed his talent in full flower.

Where does a Mozart come from? On one hand, Mozart was born into a musical family. His father, Leopold, was leader of the local orchestra and wrote an important book about violin playing. His older sister, Nannerl, was also a very talented musician in her own right. On the other hand, Mozart lucked out in his early experiences. His father devoted himself to teaching Mozart and his sister about music. At a young age, the children began traveling around Europe to perform. This gave them a chance to meet famous composers and hear the best music of their day. So the question remains: Is a Mozart born or made?

Of course, you don't have to be a genius to wonder where your intelligence comes from. In fact, scientists have spent years debating this point. How much of your intelligence is due to nature (the genes you inherit from your parents)? And how is much is due to nurture (the way you are raised and the experiences you have)?

The answer seems to be that both are important. They affect each other, too. Take going to school, for example. The amount of brainpower someone is born with influences how easily and quickly the person learns. This, in turn, may affect whether the person chooses to finish high school or go on to college. However, the number of years someone stays in school can actually change the person's IQ as well. A Swedish study showed this clearly. In the study, thousands of boys were given an IQ test at age thirteen. Five years later, more than 4,600 of the boys were tested again. The researchers found that, for every year of high school not finished, the boys' IQ scores dropped an average of two points.

> ### Growing Older and Wiser
> It's a myth that you're either smart or not and that there's nothing you can do to change things. In fact, just believing in your own ability to grow smarter can make a big difference. Research has shown that kids who believe intelligence can change tend to adjust better to middle school than those who don't. Many bright kids, in particular, find it easy to ace elementary school. When they get to middle school, though, they may have to try harder to keep getting good grades. Those who think being smart is something that just happens may give up. On the other hand, kids who work hard at getting smarter are more likely to succeed. In the words of Thomas Edison, "Genius is 1 percent inspiration and 99 percent perspiration."

You Can't Pick Your Parents

Intelligence tends to run in families, whether the name is Mozart or Jones. There are many individual exceptions to this rule. In general, though, people in the same family tend to be more alike in IQ scores than people who aren't related. In addition, the more closely related two people are, the more alike their scores are apt to be.

Animal Intelligence: Not Just Human Nature

Intelligence is part of our human nature. However, it's something other animals have to one degree or another, too. Take Alex, a famous African gray parrot. For more than twenty years, Irene Pepperberg, a researcher at the University of Arizona, has been working with Alex.

Everyone knows parrots can "talk" by simple imitation. This bird is different. He can make requests and give answers in a way that seems to show he actually understands what he's saying. Alex can identify objects, shapes, colors, and materials—not bad for a birdbrain!

In a typical exercise, Pepperberg shows Alex a tray crowded with objects. She picks up a block and asks, "What toy?" Alex replies, "Block." He then answers more questions about the object, including what shape and color it is, and what material it is made of. At times, he even seems to talk about his feelings. When he appears frustrated after making a mistake, he sometimes says, "I'm gonna go away." Then he turns his back much the way a pouting child might.

Alex is just one bird, but he offers a glimpse at the surprising mental abilities other animals may have. He also might teach us a thing or two about human intelligence. For example, the same training method that Pepperberg uses to teach new words to parrots may also help children who have trouble using language and relating well to others. With parrots, two human trainers talk back and forth while the bird looks on. Eventually, the parrot starts to chime in as a way of getting attention.

The same approach may work with children. For example, one study included seven young children with autism. Autism is a brain disorder that severely affects a person's ability to communicate with and relate to others. The children first watched two adults talking to each other in an office. Later, the children watched an adult and a child playing together on a playground. By copying what they saw, the children eventually learned how to speak and play normally with other people.

To find out more about Alex, visit the Alex Foundation online at www.alexfoundation.org. There is also a fascinating book called *Alex and Friends: Animal Talk, Animal Thinking*, by Dorothy Hinshaw Patent.

Of course, part of this might be due to growing up in the same home and having lots of experiences in common. However, part of it also seems to be due to sharing many of the same genes. Your genes are the chemical material that passes inherited traits from parent to child. Half of your genes come from your mother and half from your father. Even with the same parents, though, the mix of genes varies from child to child. Brothers and sisters share about half of the same genetic material.

There is one special case: identical twins. Such twins occur when a single egg from the mother is fertilized by one sperm from the father, and the resulting embryo splits in two at a very early stage. Since the twins started out as one, they have exactly the same genes.

A fascinating study called the Minnesota Study of Twins Reared Apart brought together as adults a number of identical twins who had been separated as children. These twins had the same genes but had grown up in different families. The twins were given several tests of mental ability. The researchers found that identical twins who had lived apart most of their lives were likely to have similar test scores. In fact, their scores were almost as similar as those of identical twins who had been raised together.

This study and others like it show that genes play a significant role in intelligence. In fact, let's say you have a large group of people with a wide range of IQ scores. Studies have shown that about half of the differences in these scores will be due to genetics. Of course, this also means that half of the differences will be due to other things. In addition, what is true for a group of people isn't always true for a particular person. In the Minnesota study, for example, one pair of twins was almost 30 points apart in IQ. This is a big enough spread to make the difference between being mentally retarded and having average intelligence. For these particular twins, something besides genes was affecting their IQ scores.

Genes That Fit

In 1999, scientists at Princeton University published an intriguing study. The scientists first bred mice with extra copies of a certain gene. This gene helps brain cells communicate with each other. Then the mice were tested in a lab on several tasks. Compared to normal mice, they learned more quickly, remembered what they had learned longer, and adapted to changes more easily. Upon hearing the news, some people thought a "smart gene" had been found. Unfortunately, it's not that simple. There is much more to intelligence than the easy tasks these mice performed. Also, any trait as complex as intelligence probably involves a large number of genes. This study is still important because it singled out a gene that may play a key role. Still, that gene is just one piece of a bigger puzzle.

You *Can* Change Your Mind

Today, most scientists believe that your genes and your experiences work together to form your intelligence. To understand this, consider the game of basketball. Since the 1940s, the popularity of the game has skyrocketed in the United States. During this time, the "basketball IQ" of Americans has increased greatly, too. Their "basketball genes" didn't change. However, people began to practice and play the game more. The coaching also improved. In addition, good players had more chances to challenge themselves on college and professional teams. All these things combined with physical capability to create more able players. In the same way, studying hard, having good teachers, and taking challenging classes can work together with mental capability to create more able students.

Some of the factors that affect intelligence are beyond your control. For example, you didn't get to choose the medical care your mother got while she was pregnant or the type of diet you ate as a young child. However, many of the choices you make for yourself today can actually affect your intelligence. That's good news, because it means you can make yourself smarter with wise choices. Of course, the reverse also is true: Poor choices can make you dumber. Here are some ways to make the most of your brainpower:

- Don't abuse alcohol. Studies have shown that heavy drinkers have smaller, lighter, more shrunken brains than other people of the same age and sex. Some of the shrinking occurs in parts of the brain used for thought and memory. Heavy drinkers may have trouble learning new information, reacting quickly, paying attention, solving problems, and forming new memories.
- Don't abuse drugs. Like alcohol, drugs can change the way your brain works. In some cases, the damage can last your entire life. Take marijuana, for example. Heavy or daily use of marijuana affects the parts of the brain that control memory and attention.

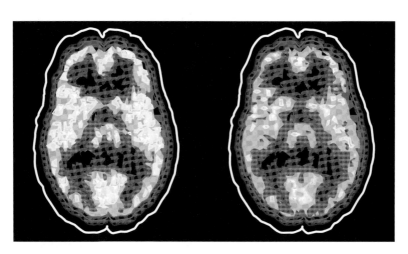

These PET scans show the brain of a normal person (left) and of a person on cocaine (right). Many areas of the brain shown at right do not use glucose, an energy source for neurons, effectively.

- Eat a healthy diet. Good nutrition helps your whole body work better, including your brain. In several studies, one group of children was given vitamins, while another group got pills that looked like vitamins but were fakes. Those who got the real thing showed greater gains in test scores than those who didn't. Of course, you could go for the same results simply by eating a diet full of vitamin-rich foods.
- Get regular exercise. Aerobic exercise refers to activities that cause you to feel warm, sweat, and breathe a little harder than usual. Examples include running, fast walking, riding a bike, or swimming laps. Such activities are good for your heart, lungs, and overall health. They're also great for your brain. They increase the amount of oxygen the brain gets, which is critical. Although the brain makes up only about 2 percent of a person's body weight, it uses 20 percent of the body's oxygen supply.
- Stay mentally active. It helps to give your brain regular workouts, too. Follow your interests and surround yourself with fascinating people. It will certainly make your life more fun. Not only that, research in rats suggests that it may be possible to literally build up your brain. Several studies have looked at rats raised in a rich environment with lots of things to respond to and

to do. These lucky rats actually grow brains that are more complex than rats raised in a boring environment. So start flexing your mind! You just might pump up your brainpower.

Your Maturing Mind

While some scientists have looked at the factors that help intelligence grow, others have focused on the stages children pass through as their minds develop. One of the most famous scientists in this field was the Swiss psychologist Jean Piaget. In 1919, Piaget took a job developing the French version of a British intelligence test. While doing this work, he noticed that children tended to give the same kinds of wrong answers at certain ages. He began to wonder about changes in the children's thinking styles as they grew older. This became the central focus of his life's work. Eventually, Piaget came to believe that children pass through four stages:

The *sensorimotor period* lasts from birth to about two years old. During this stage, children learn through their senses and by physical activity. For young babies, things that are out of sight are literally out of mind. They only seem to think about things they can see. Toward the end of this period, babies begin to realize that something exists even when the object is no longer in view.

The *preoperational period* lasts from about two to seven years old. During this stage, children become capable of thinking without doing. They are able to use language, solve some simple problems in their head, and use make-believe in their play. However, they think of everything only from their own point of view. They also have trouble focusing on more than one trait of an object at a time.

The *concrete operations* stage lasts from about seven to eleven years old. During this stage, children start to think logically. They know that when water is poured from a short, fat glass into a tall, skinny glass, the amount of water stays the same. They also notice differences in classes of objects. For example, a three-year-old child sees every dog as a "doggie." However, an eight-year-old child sees the differences between a collie and a poodle.

The *formal operations* stage lasts from about eleven to fifteen years old. During this stage, young people are finally able to think about things outside their own experience. They are ready to consider tough questions, such as "Is it wrong to steal food to feed your starving family?" or "What would happen if the sun ceased to exist?" At this stage, young people begin to think deeply about issues such as the nature of life and love, the difference between right and wrong, and their plans for the future.

Piaget's ideas have had an enormous impact on psychology and education. Still, some of his beliefs have been challenged by scientists. For one thing, some studies have suggested that babies may be capable of more complex thinking than Piaget believed. For another thing, it seems that children may pass through Piaget's stages at different speeds in different areas. For example, a child who is very strong in math might already be thinking about numbers at the formal operations level while still thinking about other things at the concrete operations level.

Then there is the chicken-and-egg question. Piaget believed that development came before learning. Once children matured to a particular point, they were able to think in a certain way about the outside world. Other scientists, including Russian psychologist Lev Vygotsky, believed that learning came before development. Once children learned from the world, their minds were ready to move on to the next stage. Put another way, Piaget believed that thinking developed from the inside out, following a pattern set by the genes. Vygotsky believed that thinking developed from the outside in, so that mental growth was prompted by children's social needs.

It all comes back to the debate over nature and nurture. There is probably some truth in both views. It takes both genes and experiences to mold something as unique and remarkable as a person's mind.

Five
Testing, Testing: The IQ Debate

The first scientific attempt to test intelligence got off to a rocky start. Francis Galton was a British scientist with a wide range of interests, including studying the weather and fingerprints. In 1884, Galton opened a service in London where people could have their intelligence checked for a small fee. Since there were no real experts in this field at the time, Galton based his test method on guesswork combined with his general science background. The only problem was his strange choice of skills to test. For example, one task used a special whistle to measure how high a pitch a person could hear. Another task involved testing how sensitive a person was to the smell of roses. Not surprisingly, his test turned out to be a scientific flop.

A French psychologist named Alfred Binet had more success. The French government asked him to come up with a way of identifying children with mental retardation so they could be given special schooling. In 1905, Binet and his partner, Theophile Simon, published a new test. It was meant to predict which students would do well in regular classes and which ones wouldn't. This was the first intelligence test that compared one child's score to that of other children. It also was the first to measure mental age—the age at which a certain level of mental ability is usually reached. Let's say a smart eight-year-old child was able to do the same tasks as an average ten-year-old child. That child was said to have a mental age of ten.

Remember Lewis Terman, the psychologist who ran the Termite study? In 1916, he translated and adapted Binet's test for use in the United States. Because he was a professor at Stanford University, the test became known as the Stanford-Binet Intelligence Scale. An updated version of this test is still in use today. To score his test, Terman borrowed an idea that had been proposed a few years earlier: the IQ. To find an IQ, Terman divided a person's mental age by his or her age in years. Then he multiplied the answer by 100. Let's take the same bright eight-year-old child with a mental age of ten. Here's how it would work:

$$(10 \div 8) \times 100 = 125$$

This is an above average IQ. Of course, most people have a mental age that is close to their age in years. Here's how it would work for an eight-year-old child with a mental age of eight:

$$(8 \div 8) \times 100 = 100$$

As you can see, an average IQ figured this way is around 100. Over the years, other intelligence tests and ways of figuring IQ have been devised. Most use a similar scale for scoring. They're set up so that about two-thirds of people get an average score between 85 and 115. Almost 15 percent of people get an above average score between 115 and 130. A similar number get a score between 85 and 70. And only a small fraction of people get a very high score above 130 or a very low score below 70.

The range of scores on an IQ test fits neatly into a bell-shaped curve. It looks like this:

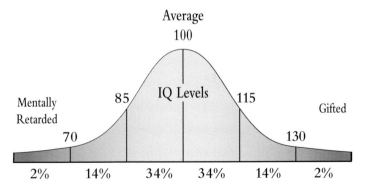

The Score on Tests

The most widely used IQ tests today are the Wechsler Intelligence Scales. These tests were developed by American psychologist David Wechsler starting in 1939. Wechsler eventually created three separate tests for different age groups. An updated form of the Wechsler Intelligence Scale for Children (WISC) is now used for young people between the ages of six and sixteen. There also are different versions of the test for younger children and for adults.

Other tests can be taken by a group of people all at once. However, the WISC, like the Stanford-Binet, is taken by just a single person at a time. This requires a lot of one-on-one attention from the specially trained person giving the test. As a result, the WISC usually is given only to students who need extra testing, rather than to everyone in a class. One reason some students take the WISC is to find out who may need to be in a special-education or gifted program. Another reason is to see if mental retardation might be the cause of behavior that seems much too young for a person's age.

IQ tests, such as the Stanford-Binet and WISC, are one type of aptitude test. An aptitude test is designed to measure a person's potential to do things. The goal is to predict how well that person will perform in the future. IQ tests are supposed to measure a person's potential to think and learn. So what do they predict? That's still an open question. Of course, the original goal of Binet's test was to predict how well children would fare in school. Today, this is still what IQ tests do best. In general, students who get high IQ scores tend to get good grades. However, let's say you have a large group of students. Only about one-fourth of the differences in school performance among the individual students will be due to IQ. This means that about three-fourths of the differences will be due to other things. Hard work, good teachers, and a strong interest in school count for a lot.

When it comes to predicting success outside of school, IQ scores are even less valuable. Some people have tried to link IQ to an individual's ability to land a good job, perform well in it, and earn a high income. In general, though, they have found that IQ scores account for only about one-tenth of the differences in job performance among people. This means that a whopping nine-tenths of the differences aren't explained by IQ.

There is an old saying: "I can is more important than IQ." As you can see, this seems to be true. IQ offers a rough idea of what a person's mental potential may be. However, it is up to each person to choose how he or she will use that potential.

What's in the WISC?

The WISC is a two-part test. One part is a verbal subtest, or part of a test, that is much like the Stanford-Binet; it relies heavily on word skills. The other part is a performance subtest that relies more on other kinds of skills, such as fitting puzzle pieces together and copying patterns. The whole test takes about 50 to

Verbal Subtest	
Task	What You Do
Information	Answer questions about well-known people, places, and events
Comprehension	Answer questions about everyday problems
Arithmetic	Solve arithmetic problems in your head
Vocabulary	Tell what certain words mean
Similarities	Tell how two things are alike
Digit span	Repeat a list of numbers forward and backward

70 minutes for the ten main tasks. It takes another 10 to 15 minutes if three optional tasks are done. Here are the particular tasks that make up each subtest (those in the white boxes are optional):

Performance Subtest	
Task	What You Do
Object assembly	Fit puzzle pieces together
Block design	Copy patterns with red and white colored cubes
Picture arrangement	Put drawings in an order that tells a logical story
Picture completion	Tell what is missing from drawings of common objects
Coding	Use a key to write symbols below the numbers they go with
Mazes	Solve paper-and-pencil mazes
Symbol search	Mark whether a given symbol appears in a list of symbols

> ### The Land of the Rising IQ
>
> It's a fact that's strange but true: IQ scores are on the rise worldwide. In fact, they have gone up several points with each new generation. This steady increase is called the Flynn effect, after New Zealand political scientist James Flynn, who first noted the trend. IQ tests are continually updated. If children today were to take an IQ test from the 1930s, at least one-quarter would score in the gifted range—ten times more than would score that high on a current test. And if children from the 1930s were scored by today's standards, a similar fraction would rate as mentally retarded.
>
> No one really thinks we're that much smarter than our grandparents. One possible explanation is that, thanks to advances such as television and computers, we live in a more complex world today. This may have caused us to develop more complex thinking skills, which has led to better test performance.

IQ tests look at general thinking ability. Another type of test looks more specifically at the kinds of word and number skills used in school. The Scholastic Aptitude Test, or SAT, is one well-known example. This is a test taken each year by more than one million high-school seniors. The goal is to help predict which students are likely to do well in college. Along with students' grades in high school, SAT scores often play a big role in deciding who gets into college and who doesn't. Yet the SAT, like any single test, is limited. It doesn't tell colleges anything about how hard a given student will study or how talented he or she is in other areas.

The Stanford-Binet, WISC, and SAT are all standardized tests. This means they are given and scored under the same conditions for everyone. Before you ever take this kind of test, it has been tried out on a large number of people. On test day, you get the same kinds of questions in the same form as all the other test takers. The instructions and time limits are the same as well. In addition, there is little or no room for judgment in how your answers are graded. The same standard is applied to everyone. Even the way your score is reported to your parents or the school is the same for all students. The big plus to this type of test, for both you and the school, is that your individual results can be compared to those of a larger group. This means standardized tests can be used to see how your skills stack up against a national sample of students.

You are probably familiar with yet another type of standardized test: the achievement test. These tests are taken in a group at school. Typically, whole classes of students take the tests each year or in certain grades. Widely used examples include the California Achievement Tests, the Iowa Tests of Basic Skills, and the Stanford Achievement Test. This kind of test measures how much a person already knows about a particular school subject. The goal is to find out what the person has learned in the past, not what he or she is likely to learn in the future. In theory, achievement tests don't measure general intelligence. In practice, though, how much someone knows is closely tied to how smart that person is. It turns out that achievement tests given in high school predict college grades about as well as the SAT does.

Test Uses and Abuses

Many people find test scores reassuring. They seem to sum up something as confusing as intelligence in one simple, neat number. In addition, the whole point of standardizing tests is to make them fair. The aim is to give everyone an equal shot at success. Such tests seem to offer a scientific solution to the problem of bias.

If this sounds far too easy, it is. In fact, IQ scores have been misused to justify all kinds of false ideas. One of the worst is the notion that differences in the average scores of different races mean that some races are smarter by nature than others. In truth, it's likely that many tests aren't as fair as they look. As one example, some kids grow up speaking a language other than English. Others learn a form of the English language at home that is quite different from the standard form taught in school. In either case, these kids may not perform up to their true ability on a word-based test. As another example, kids from cultures that stress taking your time may not do their best on a test with a time limit.

> ### The Mental Melting Pot
> *People's mental abilities are formed, in part, by the culture in which they grow up. Psychologist Robert Sternberg and his partners designed a test for children in a rural village of Kenya. The test measured the children's skill at a task that is important to them: using herbal medicines to treat illnesses. Children in the village knew the names of many such medicines—a test even the smartest kid in your class would undoubtedly flunk. The Kenyan children also were given standard IQ tests. The higher their vocabulary scores on the IQ tests, the worse their scores tended to be on the herb test. Sternberg thinks this reflects the values of the parents. Some parents stressed the native culture more, while others stressed a Western education. The children picked up these values, which shaped the mental skills they developed.*

There are probably other factors at work as well. For example, poor kids of any race may not have the same life experiences as children from middle-class homes. Yet it's just these kinds of experiences that are tapped by many questions on IQ tests. For instance, a typical question might ask a child to state what part is missing from a drawing of a bicycle. A child who has never had a bicycle of his or her own is less likely to know the answer.

Race and social class aren't the only factors that matter, of course. There are many other reasons why an IQ test might not reveal a person's true intelligence. Maybe the person was distracted by an argument on the test day, or maybe the person was sick. Perhaps the person just didn't care about the test, or simply didn't try to do well because he or she thought it was hopeless. Or maybe someone is the creative type who simply sees things differently than most people. This kind of person might come up with more than one answer for a question, rather than the single answer that is counted as correct.

The truth is, actions speak louder than test scores. What really counts are the things you *do*, not your potential for doing them. IQ tests can help identify your mental strengths and weaknesses. They also can help you see how your mental skills compare to those of a large group of people. But they still only scratch the surface of who you are. They don't show how hard you work or how eager you are to learn. They don't show how good you are at writing stories, playing basketball, or making friends. And most important, they don't say a thing about your value as a person. In the long run, it's up to you, not a mere number, to shape your life.

Glossary

achievement test: a test that measures how much a person knows about a particular subject

aptitude test: a test that is designed to measure a person's potential to do certain things

bodily-kinesthetic intelligence: the ability to use the mind to coordinate the body's movements

emotional intelligence: the ability to know and handle your own feelings and goals; it also involves dealing with other people and understanding their feelings

g: short for general factor—the single, broad mental capability that makes up general intelligence

genes: the chemical material that passes inherited traits from parent to child

giftedness: the capability for high performance in one or more key areas

intelligence: the ability to learn and then put that learning to good use

interpersonal intelligence: the ability to understand the feelings and goals of other people

intrapersonal intelligence: the ability to understand your own feelings and goals

IQ: Short for intelligence quotient; the score received on a standard test of intelligence

linguistic intelligence: the ability to use words well

logical-mathematical intelligence: the ability to think logically and use numbers well

mental age: the age at which a certain level of mental ability usually is reached mental retardation: a disorder in which intelligence, as measured by an IQ test, is well below average

multiple intelligences: a theory that expands the idea of intelligence to include not just language abilities and number skills but also other kinds of "intelligences"

musical intelligence: the ability to recognize and create musical pitches, tones, and rhythms

naturalist intelligence: the ability to recognize different plants and animals

PET scan: Short for positron-emission tomography; an image that shows the brain in action

practical intelligence: the ability to understand and solve real-life problems

spatial intelligence: the ability to create mental images in order to solve problems

standardized test: a test that is given and scored under the same conditions for everyone

Further Resources

Books

Barrett, Susan L. *It's All in Your Head: A Guide to Understanding Your Brain and Boosting Your Brain Power.* Minneapolis: Free Spirit Publishing, 1992.
A terrific book about intelligence, problem solving, memory, creativity, and more.

Burns, Marilyn. *The Book of Think (or How to Solve a Problem Twice Your Size).* Boston: Little, Brown and Company, 1976.
A book filled with tips on sharpening your thinking skills and improving your problem-solving abilities.

Galbraith, Judy, and Jim Delisle. *The Gifted Kids' Survival Guide: A Teen Handbook,* rev. ed. Minneapolis: Free Spirit Publishing, 1996.
A wonderful book written for gifted teenagers but loaded with great information for everyone.

Gilbert, Sara Dulaney. *How to Do Your Best on Tests,* rev. ed. New York: Beech Tree, 1998.
A book that offers helpful tips on taking all kinds of tests, including standardized ones.

Hancock, Jonathan. *How to Be a Genius.* Danbury: Franklin Watts, 2001.
A fun book that offers sound advice on boosting your brainpower.

Rowan, Pete. *Big Head! A Book about Your Brain and Your Head.* New York: Alfred A. Knopf, 1998.
A book filled with interesting facts about the brain and how it works.

Organizations

American Psychological Association
750 First St. NE
Washington, DC 20002-4242
(800) 374-2721
www.apa.org
Most scientists who study intelligence are psychologists. This Web site has information about the latest research on the subject.

College Board
45 Columbus Ave.
New York, NY 10023-6992
(212) 713-8000
www.collegeboard.com
This is the group that gives the SAT. Its Web site includes a practice test with real SAT questions that you can take online.

Educational Resources Information Center
Clearinghouse on Disabilities and Gifted Education
1110 N. Glebe Rd.
Arlington, VA 22201-5704
(800) 328-0272
www.ericec.org
This government center has information on gifted and special education. It covers giftedness, mental retardation, and learning disabilities.

Mensa International
1229 Corporate Dr. West
Arlington, TX 76006-6103
(800) 666-3672
www.mensa.org
This is a worldwide club for people who score in the top 2 percent of the population on a standard intelligence test. The

Web site has links to the national groups and an online quiz that is meant strictly for fun, not for testing IQ.

National Association for Gifted Children
1707 L St. NW, Suite 550
Washington, DC 20036-4212
(202) 785-4268
www.nagc.org
This is a group for parents and teachers who are interested in gifted education. The Web site has a list of special programs for gifted kids.

National Center for Fair and Open Testing (FairTest)
342 Broadway
Cambridge, MA 02139
(617) 864-4810
www.fairtest.org
This group aims to fight abuses, misuses, and flaws in standardized testing.

Other

British Mensa Limited. *Mensa for Kids* cards. San Francisco: Chronicle Books, 1997. One set of cards features word puzzles to give your brain a workout. Other sets include number puzzles, brain bafflers, and secret codes.

Index

Pages in *italics* indicate illustrations.

academics and giftedness, 39
achievement test, 65–66, 69
alcohol abuse and brain power, 51
Alex (African gray parrot), 46–47
Alex and Friends: Animal Talk, Animal Thinking (Patent), 47
Alvarez, Luis, 14
animals and intelligence, 46–47
aptitude test, 60–61, 69
arithmetic. *See* mathematics
artificial intelligence, 6
arts and giftedness, 39
autism, 47

basketball, 50
Binet, Alfred, 58
bodily-kinesthetic intelligence, 11, 35, 69
brain, 9, *10*, 17, 27, 51
　images, *10*
　size, 9, 27
brainpower, 7, 50–53
　ways to make the most of, 50–53
Burke, Chris, 31–32

California Achievement Tests, 65
Carroll, John, 22–23, 26
Churchill, Winston, 33
common sense, 11, 28, 37
concrete operations, 54
creativity and giftedness, 37, 39
culture as factor in mental abilities, 11–12, 26–28, 29, 67
Czyz, Bobby, 8

daydreaming, 5, 6
diet and brainpower, 52
Dmytryk, Edward, 14
Down syndrome, 31–32
drug abuse and brainpower, 51

Edison, Thomas, 6, 45
Einstein, Albert, 27
emotional intelligence (EQ), 36, 69
excelling in school, 5, 12, 38–39, 44–45, 61
exercise and brainpower, 52
experience and intelligence, 43–55

Flynn, James, 64
formal operations, 54, 55
Frames of Mind (Gardner), 33

g factor (general factor), 17–29, 69
   assessing, 19–26
   mental pecking order, 19
   problems with tests, 26–28
   sample tests, 20–21
Galton, Francis, 57–58
Gardner, Howard, 33–35, 38
general factor. *See g* factor
general intelligence
   achievement test and, 66
   giftedness and, 39
general thinking ability, 64
genes, 44, 45, 48–51, 70
giftedness, 38–39, 70
   academics, 39
   arts, 39
   creativity, 39
   general intelligence, 39
   leadership, 39

Human Cognitive Abilities (Carroll), 22

identical twins, 48
intelligence
   definition of, 7, 28–29, 70
   genes as factor, 45, 48–51, 70
   giftedness and, 38–39
   Howard Gardner's eight types of, 34–35
   multiple intelligences, 11, 33–37, 71
   nature versus nurture, 43–55
   practical intelligence, 11, 37, 71
   three levels of, 24–25
   uncontrollable factors, 50
   ways to make the most of your brainpower, 50–53
intelligence quotient. *See* IQ
interpersonal intelligence, 11, 35, 70
intrapersonal intelligence, 35, 70
Iowa Tests of Basic Skills, 65
IQ (intelligence quotient)
   averaging, 58–59
   definition, 8–9, 70
IQ test, 33, 36, 37, 59, 60, 64, 66–68
   debate about, 57–68
   family genes and test scores, 48–49
   misusing test scores, 66–68
   rising scores, 64
   Stanford-Binet Intelligence Scale, 59
   Wechsler Intelligence Scales, 60

Jarvik, Robert, 33

Kennedy, John F., 33
Keys, Ancel, 14

laboratory mice, 49, 52–53
language and IQ scores, 8–9, 66
leadership and giftedness, 39
linguistic intelligence, 34, 36, 70
logical-mathematical intelligence, 34, 36, 70

machines, 6
marijuana and brainpower, 51
mathematics, 11, 12, 22, 25, 27, 36, 55, 62
    WISC test and, 62
    memory, 18, 23, 25, 51
Mensa, 7–8
mental abilities, 11, 12, 19, 22–23, 43
    importance of, 12
    John Carroll's eight groups of, 22–23
    maturing mind, 53–55
mental activity and brainpower, 52–53
mental age, 58, 70
mental retardation, 32, 58, 60, 64, 71

Minnesota Study of Twins Reared Apart, 48–49
Morphonios, Ellen, 8
Mozart, Leopold, 43–44
Mozart, Nannerl, 44
Mozart, Wolfgang Amadeus, 43–44
multiple intelligences, 11, 33–37, 71
musical intelligence, 11, 34, 71
myths about intelligence, 6, 7–12, 41, 45

naturalist intelligence, 35, 71
nature and intelligence, 43–55
Newton, Isaac, 33

Oppenheimer, Jess, 14

Patent, Dorothy Hinshaw, 47
Pepperberg, Irene, 46
PET scan, 9, 71
Piaget, Jean, 53–55
Plato, 18
positron-emission tomography. *See* PET scan
practical intelligence, 11, 37, 40–41, 71
    Robert Sternberg's tips, 40–41
preoperational period, 54

Princeton University study, 49
problem-solving abilities, 18

races and IQ scores, 66
reading, 11, 36
robots, 6

SAT (Scholastic Aptitude Test), 64–65, 66
sensorimotor period, 53
Shockley, William, 14
Simon, Theophile, 58
"smart gene", 49
social class and IQ scores, 67–68
spatial intelligence, 34, 71
Spearman, Charles, 17–18
standardized test, 65, 66, 67, 71
Stanford Achievement Test, 65
Stanford-Binet Intelligence Scale, 59, 60, 61, 62, 65
Sternberg, Robert, 37, 40–41, 67
Stone, Sharon, 8
"street smarts", 11, 37
Successful Intelligence (Sternberg), 40

Terman, Lewis, 13, 58
"Termites" study, 13–15, 58

vocabulary, 18, 22, 62, 67
   WISC test and, 62
Vygotsky, Lev, 55

Washington, George, 33
Wechsler, David, 60
Wechsler Intelligence Scales, 60
WISC (Wechsler Intelligence Scale for Children), 60–65
   performance subtest, 63
   verbal subtest, 62
writing, 11, 36

About the Author

Linda Wasmer Andrews learned to read and write at a young age, so she got the "smart kid" label early in school. She didn't turn out to be all that smart about a lot of things; to this day she can't catch a ball, read a map, or set the time on her DVD player. However, she did become a busy writer. She is the author of five books and more than 1,700 book chapters, magazine and newsletter articles, and Web pages. Her specialty is writing about psychology, health, and the mind-body connection. Linda lives in Albuquerque, New Mexico, with her husband. She has a bachelor's degree in psychology from the University of New Mexico.

The author thanks the following people, who kindly shared their knowledge and insights about key subjects:

Eric Chown, Ph.D., computer scientist, Bowdoin College (artificial intelligence)

Hendrie Weisinger, Ph.D., psychologist (emotional intelligence)

Parents and kids from the GT-Families e-mailing list (gifted students)